MACRAMÉ FOR BEG.

An illustrated and easy guide with creative ideas to improve your home and garden. Knot, projects, and modern patterns for beginners

ALESSIA ORTIZ

Table of Contents

Introduction

When you need to decorate your home, can't afford a lot of fancy wallpaper, or just want to spruce up a room, macramé is a great way to add a unique flair to your décor.

You don't need any specialized tools or skills in order to do macramé. All you need is some rope, some hooks and scrapbook paper. It's easy and fun for the whole family.

Macramé is a type of craft that involves stringing beads or materials together and manipulating them into specific patterns. Historically, macramé has been used to make jewelry and other decorative items, especially for women. Today, people of all ages use macramé to create a wide range of utilitarian and artistic items: wreaths, belts, purses, storage bags, etc.

While it's commonly thought that macramé involves only bead crafting, it can be done with string or fabric. In fact, it's possible to work string with beads as well! Since beads are fairly inexpensive and easily found at craft and hobby stores, they are the most popular material for beginners and seasoned macramé artists. However, there are other materials that more experienced artists enjoy working with.

It is said that the best kind of art is the kind that is made by children. This is precisely what makes macramé so appealing. Here are a few reasons why people love it:

- It can be a great way to introduce your kids to different types of art
- It helps them learn how to create their own artwork with simple, yet creative materials
- It is portable and can be taken on the go
- It makes a great keepsake for your kids later in life

Macramé is a classic craft that requires no special skills or tools. It is an art that can be used to decorate furnishings, decorative rugs, furniture, and whatever you can imagine. With a few basic tools and a calm hand, you can soon be creating art that will add style and comfort to your home.

What are the different kinds of macramé?

There are two basic kinds of macramé, plus a third method called tatting.

Handmade macramé is made from waxed linen thread and embroidery floss. This kind of work can be fairly easy to learn because it does not require any special or difficult-to-find materials.

Beading is made with beads (usually glass), but the same finished effect could be obtained just as easily with seed beads or small metal crystals. This kind of work will take more practice before you can produce the finished result you want.

Tatting is a comparatively more difficult type of work. It requires special materials and much more time and patience than macramé. Yet it produces the same result in the end, so it's worth learning!

Personal satisfaction is what drives our team. We design with this in mind. We make sure our products are easy to use, durable, and functional. When you choose a tool from macramé, you will be using a reliable product that will serve you for years to come.

Our products are simple to use but will last for years of comfortable work. Whether you're crafting with leather, canvas, rope, or wire, we have the tools to get the job done. With durable material in your choice of colors, you can complete any project no matter how challenging it may be. When you buy a tool from macramé, you can allow yourself time to enjoy the process so that you can be sure that your projects will be well thought out and executed with pride.

It's a fairly simple process, and if you've never attempted macramé before, it does require some practice. First, you need to figure out a design. You can do this in several ways:

- Look at a pattern. Choose one of the designs we have online or pick your own.
- Draw a design on an old t-shirt or something similar.
- Experiment with different shapes and sizes until you figure out what works for you.

Once you're done creating your design, you'll want to completely cover it up with macramé. The best way to do this is to use one strand for each stitch and wind the strands together, making sure to leave extra rope (called 'floating') of about 2 inches or so. You can tie the ends together in an overhand knot or simply pull them through the center of the knot. Make sure that all of your knots are tight enough so that no new strands can be added, but not so tight that they become too difficult to untie later. Once these knots are secured, you're ready for the next step: pulling apart the loops to form your shape. This part is a bit tricky! The key is to pull enough so that all of the strands in your pattern are wrapped around each other in the same direction. You can use scissors if necessary, but they're not necessary for most designs. Just make sure that when you cut your strands apart, all of them have the same direction of travel—from top to bottom, or vice versa (depending on what you started with). As long as this is done correctly, your knot will be perfectly round and perfect for hanging on the wall or for other purposes! If you've successfully managed this process, then congratulations! You've just completed macramé!

Chapter 1: Tools and Materials needed

There are several recognized fabrics used to do macramé. These include silk, rayon, raffia threads, shoe sewing threads, cotton threads, jute, cloth strips, leather strips, shoelace, and all other lightweights, malleable, foldable, and durable and hand safe fabrics. Yet jute, silk, linen, and cotton are the most common fabrics used for macramé as they tie easily, come in several sizes, can be dyed, and are readily available. Any yarns come with wax, creosote, or scale finish on them. Besides, any material is suitable for macramé, which can be bought in incredible lengths and seems to be pliable. Jute, raffia, cotton, and rayon threads are indigenous to the materials described above.

The possible origins of macramé's were linen, hemp, and jute, and other fabrics, which were mainly used for clothing and nets. As travelers and merchants collected various forms of material from the territories they traveled, they helped build the art and move it on. Fast-forward to the modern-day, when we have emerging technology, fabrics, and most importantly, the Internet, and you have the most incredible array of materials, beads, and findings to produce just about everything you can picture.

Nevertheless, macramé requires more than just yarn, findings, and beads. Many of the materials that you'll need to create the designs you probably already own. You can easily purchase something you don't have onboard at your nearest art shop or, in certain situations, even your nearest hardware store.

Cords

If you can make a knot into it, you should possibly use it to macramé. Waxed hemp and Waxed-linen are two of the most popular fibers used for working macramé. The wax covering on such strings helps them hold a tie extraordinarily well. Your ties and the following knot patterns will be very well defined. Art shops and beads sell those cords, or you can quickly find them in online stores.

Another common macramé fabric is Rattail, a satin cord that comes in a colored spectrum and with at least three distinct sizes. In the late 70s, Rattail was common but never gone out of style with craftsmen who like to integrate Chinese Knots or Celtic Knots into their projects. It can be slick, but if not fixed properly, the knots tied in Rattail will loosen. But the results look so amazing that it is worth using this stuff.

Linen

Linen cording comes in a broad range of colors and sizes that make it highly desirable for many styles of braiding. Linen does have the durability and range that most other cording materials don't have, making it ideal for macramé projects that need to be sturdy and robust. Linen cording is mostly used in wall hangings in macramé and looks fantastic when paired with other cording types, such as cotton and silk. The only thing to keep in mind while working with linen cording is that it will unravel very quickly, so one needs to be very sure to finish the project's ends cautiously.

Cotton

Cotton threads are weaker than jute, hemp, or linen and need more bending to allow them to hold together to form a chain. In most fabric and sewing shops, where you work, you can purchase cotton cording or even from weaving suppliers. Single-ply cotton is used for macramé creations that you'll wear, like a shirt. Cotton cording tends to come in a wide range of sizes and is found in many designs of macramé.

Chinese Cord

This woven nylon cord preserves its circular form while it is running. The thinner cords, which are presently available in 0.4–3 mm, are usually more common with macramé. Look for the largest color options available online, although you may note the color choices for the thicker cords are not as comprehensive as those for the thinner cords.

Satin

This velvety string has bright shine and is accessible in a range of sizes: the bug tail is 1 mm in diameter, the mousetail is 1.5 mm in thickness, and the rattail is 2 mm, but in fact, it is now labeled as rattail. The string is relatively lightweight, and it does not help very much the form of the ties, which is not very hard-wearing.

Paracord

This curvy cord typically comes in two diameters: paracord 550 (4 mm) has 7 strands down the middle, and paracord 450 (2 mm) has 4 middle strings. Paracord is ideal for creating bracelets and some other items with individual knots and is famous for male jewelry because it is very thick. The cord is available in a wide variety of dark and bright solid colors and in several multicolored designs.

Embroidery Threads

Stranded cotton and perlé cotton are only two easily accessible fibers that can be used in macramé. Embroidery threads are fragile and do not keep a knot's form tightly, but when paired with tougher cords, they look fine. The variety of colors is much wider than with other strings, and thrilling color combinations are likely. Although embroidery threads are normally matte, a bit of shimmer can be applied for shiny embroidery threads.

Leather Thong

Circular leather thong, because it is a strong string, makes a nice distinct knot. It comes in a variety of diameters from around 0.5 mm up to 6 mm. The thinner cords are ideal for tying knots, and the thicker cords are best fit for use as filler for winding the knots around. Leather thong comes in natural colors and a wide array of colors. Pearlescent finishes are especially appealing, typically in light pastels, as are the various thicknesses of the snakeskin result cords.

Wire

The wire is a challenging resource to use for macramé—but if you learn the craft, the results can be extremely special pieces of jewelry. The nature of metal is not to turn over and over again. This loses strength, so repetitive bending allows the wire to become fragile, so work-hardened. When you turn it back and forth, again and again, it will finally crack. The thicker wire doesn't turn without a huge deal of energy. Many metal macramé are made from thinner diameter wire, which is simpler to manipulate. When it's worked, it will still tighten, so the less you fold it, the best.

Necessary Tools

Macramé Boards

Macramé projects have to be fastened to a surface as you work, usually using a T pin or masking tape. It makes it easier to work with the cords, and it also helps to keep the ties secure and correctly positioned. In the nearest craft store or bead, or from online stores, specifically made macramé frames are accessible, and they work for most designs. They are usually around 12 inches/18 inches (30 cm/46 cm) and built of fiberboard. Many macramé boards created have a graph on the surface and rulers along the edges. They can be replaced, but it's better to keep them in place using seals or shrink-wrapped because they can be handy directions when working on a project. Some other boards also include instructive diagrams of the basic knots in the macramé.

Tape and Pins

Pins are being used to protect the macramé board project, so it wouldn't shift about while you are working. These also come in handy when you integrate different knot patterns and other design features into your designs to keep other strings in position.

The most common alternative for macramé is t-pins. They are good in scope, and their form makes it convenient to place and remove again and again. It is also possible to use ball-end pins used for embroidery, but they are not as durable as T-pins. Resist replacing push pins and thumbtacks, which are both too small.

Scissors

Most macramé creations are composed of thin fibers that are easy to cut with a simple pair of art scissors like those you likely do own. You need to get a set of little cleaning scissors made for stitching to cut the extra length when a task is done. They'll let you get close to whatever knot you want to cut.

Adhesives

Most macramé projects are finished by securing the final knot(s) with adhesives. The type of adhesive that will be used would depend on the materials involved. Hemp, waxed linen, silk, cotton, and other fabrics are perfect for white glue. Leather and suede are ideally suited for rubber cement or touch cement. E-6000 and epoxy are very strong adhesives used to glue non-porous items together, such as labradorite beads or wire, which are used with the strap of the heart belt. Any of these adhesives require adequate airflow while in use and should be enforced strictly by all health warnings. The most favored type is the third! A powerful and durable, nontoxic, water-based super glue. Bear in mind the toxicity of the glue when choosing which glue is better to use for your project, mainly if it may come into contact with your skin.

Findings

These are all the small pieces, usually made of metal, used to create and complete jewelry items and other accessories. Some of the findings are used to conceal the things that are freshly made. Some of the findings are used to protect the rough ends of strings, so it is essential to select the proper shape and size. Keep a broad range of findings in your workbox so you can build and complete various items.

The Finishing Ends

We use these findings to finish the edges of knotted strings. There are increasing numbers of designs being produced year after year, and the majority is available in a variety of shiny textures. For better outcomes, fit the cord or braid to suit the inner measurements of the finishing ends. Some finished ends contain a clasp, but if not, you may add it yourself.

Cord Ends

This type is used to finish individual cords with lugs that you attach with clamps over the string; some are tubular and are therefore sealed with glue or by an internal crimping ring.

Spring Ends

It is one of the older finding types. It may be conical or cylindrical. Inside of the wire coil, wrap the string or braid, and use wire cutters to pinch just the end circle to seal it.

Cones End

Some cone-shaped or bell-shaped findings may either have a small hole at the top or end in a loop. Use jewelry glue to protect the braid in all designs for better results.

End Caps

End caps are rectangular, circular, or cylindrical styles of an end cone, with either a hole at the top edge or are ready-to-finish with a ring or circle. Use jewelry glue to protect the braid in all designs for better outcomes.

Trigger Clasp

This cheap spring-closure fastening is ideal for both necklaces and bracelets finishing. The lobster claw and a bolt ring are some of the available designs.

Multi-strands Fasteners

Multi-strands fasteners come in a variety of types. The box kind is perfect for necklaces, and for macramé and other cuff-style bracelets, the slider fastening is best. Select the number of rings on either side to suit your project.

Plastic Fasteners

These plastic clasps are explicitly made for knotting techniques such as crochet or macramé since they have a bar end to tie the cords. The fasteners are available in a variety of sizes and luminous colors.

Beads

Without beads, most macramé creations will not be complete. The accessible bead choices are stunning. The range of beads to deal with was small when the macramé started. Since exchange has spread across the globe and technological advances, the beads that jewelry designers have to pick from nowadays are almost limitless.

Chapter 2: Secrets and Tricks

If you are an amateur or learner of the specialty of macramé, here are some fundamental tips to assist you with keeping away from botches and be fully operational in your new interest. Hitching is the way to macramé, yet before you get moving, here are a few hints that will spare you time and dissatisfaction when you are simply beginning to learn.

Become familiar with the essential bunches with hemp line, as it is anything but difficult to work with and simple to fix ties.

When you have the fundamental macramé ties down, use nylon cording for your underlying gems ventures, as opposed to silk. It's a lot simpler to evacuate tying botches.

Searing the closures just works with nylon cording.

Make a straightforward undertaking board to use as your working territory. It's anything but difficult to make and can go anyplace, making your undertaking truly versatile.

Continuously twofold watch that the string you intend to utilize fits through the dot openings (before you start!).

To shield the finishes from fraying, tie a bunch toward the finish of the rope. You can utilize clear nail clean on the parts of the bargains to shield them from fraying too, and this additionally stiffens the closures, making it simpler to string those small seed globules. You can likewise utilize a "no quarrel" fluid found in texture stores to do a similar activity.

Spare extra bits of cording to rehearse new bunches. The way into a cleaned search for your piece is uniform tying. Careful discipline brings about promising results!

If you don't have any T nails to hand, use corsage pins to make sure about your work. If utilizing calfskin cording, make an X with two pins to make sure the line is set up so as not to cut the rope. Spot the pins on either side of the line crossing in an askew way, similar to A X to secure the string set up.

Remember that each of these knots is going to be the foundation of the other projects that you create, so you have to take the time to get familiar with each of them—and practice them until they are what you need them to be. You aren't likely going to get them perfectly right away—so take the time to make sure you do it right before you move on to the one.

Don't worry if you don't get it at first, it's going to come with time, and the more time you put into it, the better you are going to become. It does take time and effort to get it right, but the more time and effort you put into it, the better you are going to be.

But you look at the price, and you suddenly put it down. You would love to be able to support the artist, and you would love to fill your house with all kinds of handmade and unique items, but when it comes down to it, you simply can't afford to pay those kinds of prices. Of course, it is all worth it, but when you can't afford it, you can't afford it.

Yet, you don't walk away empty-handed. You now have more inspiration than you know what to do with. You want to make and create. You want to do something that is going to catch the eye of your friends and family, and you want to turn it into something that is amazing. When it comes to the world of hand-crafted items, you are going to find that there really is no end to the ways you can show off your creativity with the things that you make.

But you have the creativity and you don't know what to do with it. You want to make something, but when it comes to the actual execution of the craft, you feel lost.

And that's where this book comes in. In this book, you are going to find all kinds of new knots that you can then use to create whatever it is you want to create. You are going to find that there is no end to the ways that you can use your skills to create whatever it is you wish.

It can be difficult at first, but the more you put into it, the easier it's all going to become until it is just second nature to you. I know you are going to fall in love with each and every aspect of this hobby, and when you know how to work the knots, you are going to want to make them in all the ways you possibly can.

Don't worry about the colors, and don't worry if you don't get it right the first time. This book is going to give you everything you need to make it happen the way you want it to, and it is going to show you that you really can have it all with your macramé projects.

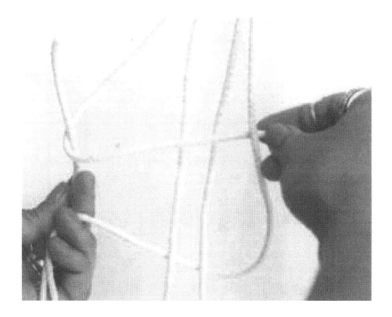

Using decent quality rope

A wide range of macramé-fitting cotton, acrylic, nylon, and twine cords with a rope-like twist are available in the art and home stores. Personally, I consider using a cotton rope at least 3 mm in diameter. Cotton clothes come in two kinds. Twisted and twisted cotton bandage. The braided

21

cotton rope is woven into one continuous rope by six (or more) threads. 3-Strand rope (sometimes called a 3-ply) where the fibers are twisted. I saw it in four strands but it seems like a typical 3-strand thread. I love it because working with it is really easy, incredibly strong, and robust, and it unravels to make a very good fringe at the ends.

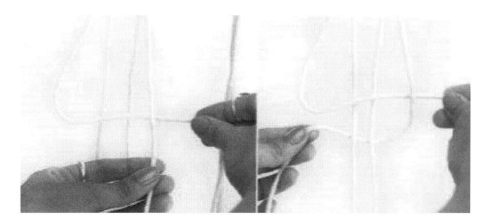

Keep it simple

There are so many different knots to use in macramé. A strong first-node is a basic node to know in a square. There are two ways of creating the node: a rectangular node, and alternates a rectangular node. The whole foundation of most the macramé out there these days is this knot, and a wonderfully easy knot for beginners to try.

Keep your tension even

This one has to be practiced. The strength with which the knots are tightened affects the consistency of their size. Practice over and over until you find a rhythm and see your knots are consistent. You're going to need to find a balance between knotting to lose and having your work look shoddy and knotting too tight.

Get involved and have fun

The easiest way to do something is to get the proper help. The same holds true for learning macramé. Join a fellow member of the amateur macramé. You will find answers to your questions, will be inspired and will share information. Expressing your imagination by macramé is one of the best parts of the voyage. Let your imagination go wild and construct something from the heart.

Attend a Workshop

Teaching yourself is fun, but we suggest you attend a workshop if you have any in your area. You get to get in touch with so many like-minded people, and even leave with not only your very own finished work of art but also new friends! We're going on a full US workshop tour this summer, where we're going to teach wall hanging, plant hangers, mobile phones, chandeliers, headpieces, and more! Check out our tour page for a city near you.

Save Your Left-Over Cord

You should make some attempts while you are training, and try again. And having the right length of just cord can be your biggest obstacle. You don't want a little string, because it can be hard to add extra to your piece. We also recommend that you make at least 10 percent more mistakes than you think you should, just to be safe.

In the new Modern Macramé book, we have a detailed step-by-step variable on how to evaluate how many ropes you need for your macramé.

That's in mind, you could end up with an extra cord at the end of your project! Not to worry about that! We recommend that you save all of your remaining strings. You can add the used cord to future projects, and if you stay tuned, we'll be launching a very special free pattern in the next few weeks, which is a fun way to reuse your scraps.

Chapter 3: Various Knots

Capuchin Knot

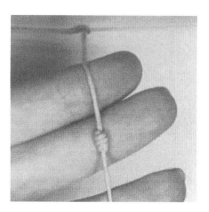

This is a knot for any project and can be used as the foundation for the base of the project. Use lightweight cord for this—it can be purchased at craft stores or online, wherever you get your macramé supplies.

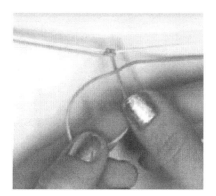

Watch the photos very carefully as you move along with this project, and take your time to make sure you are using the right string at the right point of the project.

Don't rush and make sure you have even tension throughout. Practice makes perfect, and with the illustrations to help you, you'll find it's not hard at all to create.

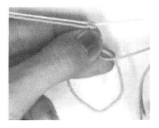

Start with the base cord, tying the knot onto this, and working your way along with the project.

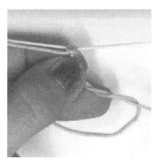

Twist the cord around itself two times, pulling the string through the center to form the knot.

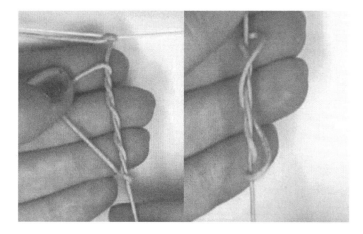

For the finished project, make sure that you have all your knots secure and firm throughout, and do your best to make sure it is all even. It is going to take practice before you are able to get it perfectly each time, but remember that practice does make perfect, and with time, you are going to get it without too much trouble.

Make sure all is even and secure, and tie off. Snip off all the loose ends, and you are ready to go!

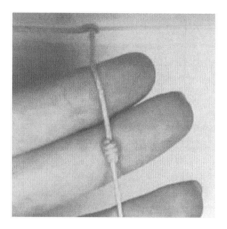

Crown Knot

This is a great beginning knot for any project and can be used as the foundation for the base of the project. Use lightweight cord for this—it can be purchased at craft stores or online, wherever you get your macramé supplies.

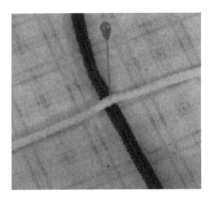

Look at the photos very carefully as you go through this project and take your time to make sure you are using the correct string at the correct point of the project.

Make sure you have even tension at all times. Remember that practice makes perfect, and with the illustrations to help you, it won't be difficult to create.

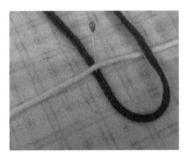

Use a pin to help keep everything in place as you are working.

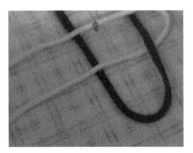

Weave the strings in and out of each other as you can see in the photos. It is helpful to practice with different colors to help you see what is going on.

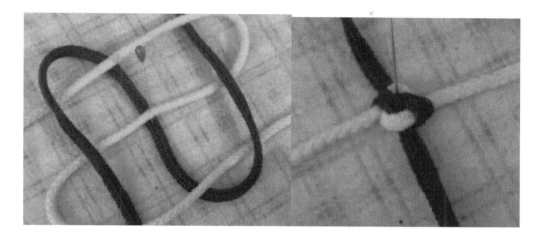

Pull the knot tight, then repeat for the next row on the outside.

Continue to do this as often as you like to create the knot. You can make it as thick as you like, depending on the project. You can also create more than one length on the same cord.

Make sure you have all your knots secure and tight at all times; everything should be even in the finished project. It will take practice before you can get it right every time, but with time, you will get it without too much trouble.

Make sure everything is even and secure, and tie off. Cut off all the loose ends, and you are ready to go!

Diagonal Double Half Knot

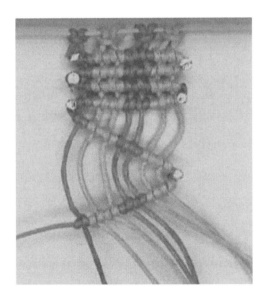

This is the perfect knot to use for basket hangings, decorations, or any projects that are going to require you to put weight on the project. Use a heavier weight cord for this, which you can find at craft stores or online.

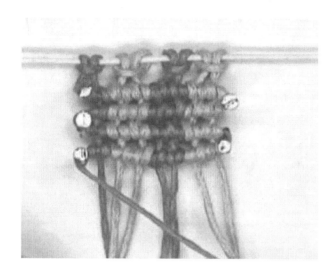

Take your time to make sure you are using the correct string at the correct point of the project and look at the photos very carefully as you go through this project.

You should make sure you have even tension at all times. Remember that practice makes perfect, and with the illustrations to help you, you won't find it difficult to create.

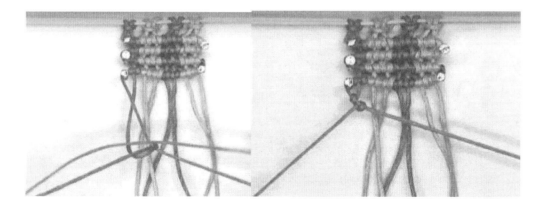

Start at the top of the project and work your way toward the bottom. Keep it even as you work your way throughout the piece. Tie the knots at 4-inch intervals, working your way down the entire piece.

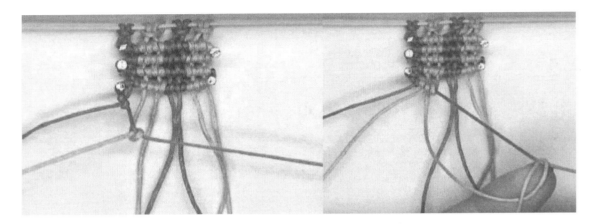

Weave in and out throughout, watching the photo as you can see for the right placement of the knots. Again, it helps to practice with different colors so you can see what you need to do throughout the piece.

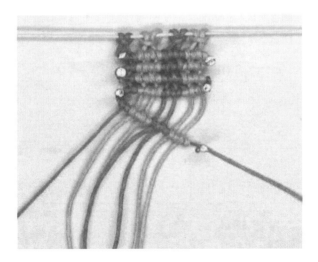

For the finished project, everything should be even. All your knots should be secure and tight at all times. It will take practice before you can get it right every time, but with time, you will get it without too much trouble.

Before the tie, make sure everything is even and secure. Cut off all the loose ends and it is ready!

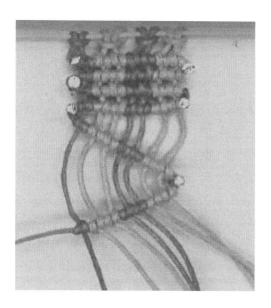

Frivolite Knot

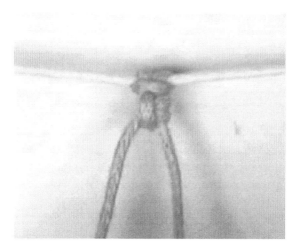

This is a great starting knot for any project and can be used as a base for the project foundation. Use lightweight cord for this—it can be purchased at craft stores or online, wherever you get your macramé supplies.

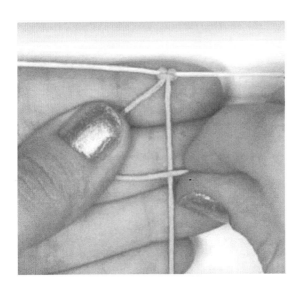

Look at the photos very carefully and take your time to make sure you are using the right string at the right point of the project.

Use the base string as the guide to hold it in place, then tie the knot onto this. This is a very straightforward knot, watch the photo and follow the directions you see.

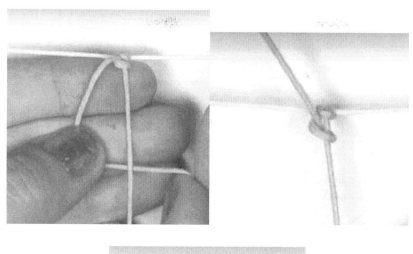

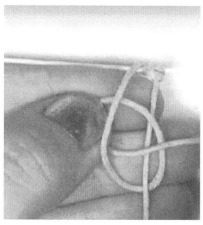

Pull the end of the cord up and through the center.

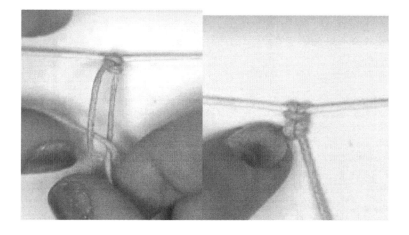

In the finished project, all your knots should be secure and tight at all times and everything should be even. Remember that practice makes perfect, and with time, you will get it without too much trouble.

Make sure everything is even and secure before tying. Cut off all the loose ends and you are ready to go!

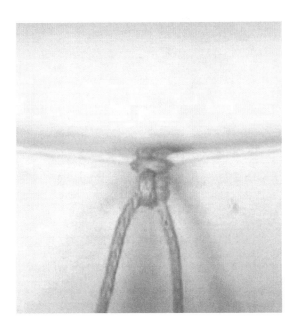

Horizontal Double Half Knot

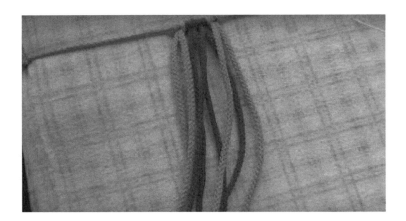

This is an excellent starting knot for any project and can be used as a base for the project. Use lightweight cord for this—it can be purchased at craft stores or online, wherever you get your macramé supplies.

As you go through this project, look at the photos very carefully and take your time to make sure you are using the correct string at the correct point of the project.

Remember that practice makes perfect, and with these illustrations to help you, it won't be hard to create. Don't rush and make sure you have even tension at all times.

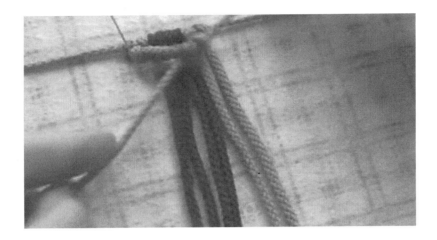

Start from the top of the project toward the bottom. As you work throughout the piece, keep it even and tie the knots at 4-inch intervals.

Everything should be even in the finished project and all your knots should be secure and tight. It will take time before you can get it right, but then you will get it done without too much trouble.

Tie off making sure everything is even and secure. Snip off all the loose ends and it is ready!

Josephine Knot

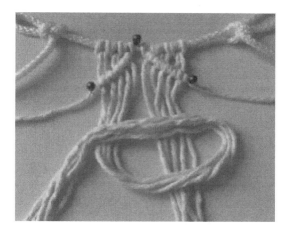

This is the perfect knot to use for basket hangings, decorations, or any projects that are going to require you to put weight on the project. Use a heavier weight cord for this, which you can find at craft stores or online.

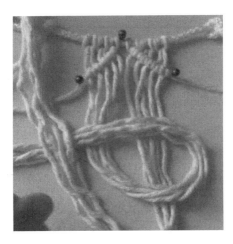

Take your time to make sure you are using the right string at the right point of the project as you go through this project. Look at the photos very carefully.

With the illustrations to help you, it won't be difficult to create. Don't rush and make sure you have even tension at all times.

Use the pins along with the knots that you are tying, and work with larger areas all at the same time. This is going to help you keep the project in place as you continue to work throughout the piece.

Pull the ends of the knots through the loops, and form the ring in the center of the strings.

Everything should be even in the finished project and all your knots should be secure and tight. It will take practice before you can get it perfect every time, but remember that practice makes perfect; with time, you will get it done without trouble.

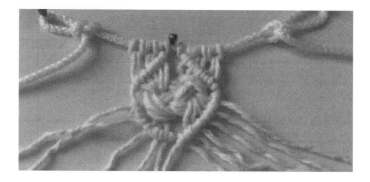

After making sure everything is even and secure, you can tie and then snip off all the loose ends!

Lark's Head Knot

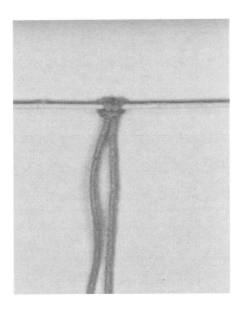

This is a fantastic starting knot for any project and can be used as the foundation for the project. Use lightweight cord for this—it can be purchased at craft stores or online, wherever you get your macramé supplies.

When you make this project, look at the photos very carefully and take your time to make sure you are using the right string at the right point of the project.

You should make sure you have even tension at all times. These illustrations will help you to find them easy to create.

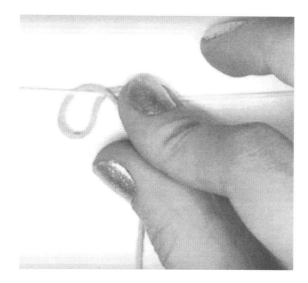

Use the base string as the core part of the knot, working around the end of the string with the cord. Make sure all is even as you loop the string around the base of the cord.

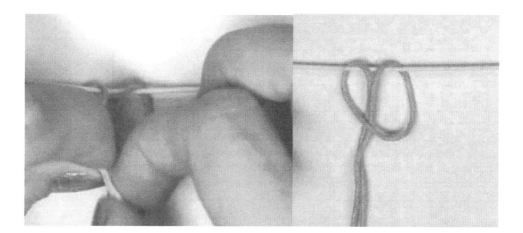

Create a slip knot around the base of the string and keep both ends even as you pull the cord through the center of the piece.

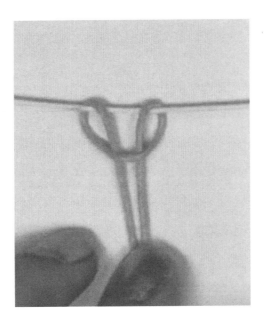

For the finished project, your knots should be secure and tight and everything even. Remember that practice makes perfect, and with time, you will get it perfectly every time.

When everything is even and secure, you can tie and then cut all the loose ends!

Reverse Lark's Head Knot

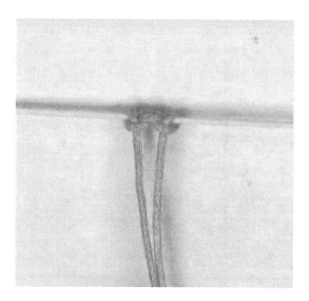

This is a perfect knot that can be used as the base for any project. Use lightweight cord for this—it can be purchased at craft stores or online, wherever you get your macramé supplies.

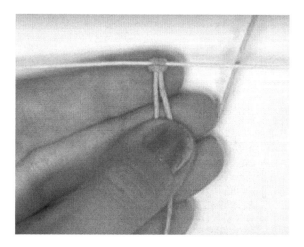

Look at the photos very carefully when you make this project and take your time to make sure you are using the right string at the right point of the project.

Remember that practice makes perfect and with these illustrations to help you, it will be easy to create. Don't rush and make sure you have even tension at all times.

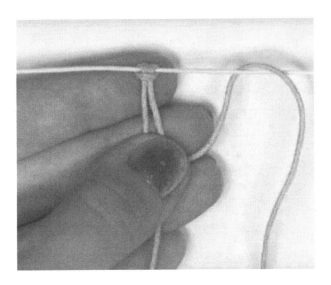

Use two hands to make sure that you have everything even and tight as you work. You can use tweezers if it helps to make it tight against the base of the string.

Crown Knot

Crown knot means that you have to go over the knot, go under twice, over twice, and under again. Use lightweight cord for this—it can be purchased at craft stores or online, wherever you get your macramé supplies.

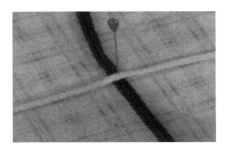

You should make sure you have even tension at all times. Remember that practice makes perfect and with these illustrations to help you, you will find it easy to create.

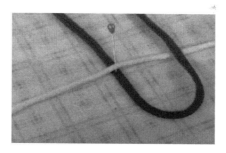

While you are working, use a pin to help keep everything in place.

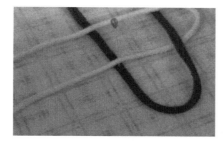

Practice with different colors will be helpful to see what is happening. Weave the strings together as you can see in the photos.

Pull the knot tight, then repeat for the row on the outside.

You can make it thick, depending on the project. You can also create more than one length on the same cord.

For the finished project, everything should be even and your knots should be secure and tight. It will take practice before you can get it perfectly every time, but with time, you will get it done without trouble.

Before tying, make sure everything is even and secure and then cut all the loose ends. You are ready to go!

Chapter 4: Initial Projects

Pet Leash

Materials to Be Used

- Swivel Hook
- Glue
- 4mm or 6mm cord material
- Project board and pins

Knots to Be Used

- Square Knots (SK)
- Wrapped Knot (WK)

- Overhand Knot
- Buttonhole Clasp
- Vertical Larks Head Knot (Vertical LHK)

Calculations

- The length of the material (Leash) after the work is done should be determined by you and, after it has been selected, you should try out this calculation.
- Length of leash (in inches) = WC /3 (in yards).
- The length of the Holding cord also increases by 0.5 yards for every 10 inches, the length of the leash is beginning from 20 inches, which is 2 yards long (i.e., 20 inches = 2 yards, 30 inches = 2.5 yards, 40 inches = 3 yards....) till you get to your desired leach's length.
- The total amount of materials needed therefore depends on this calculation.

Steps

1. Put the two cords vertically on our board after getting their corresponding midpoints and tightly place them close to each other. The longer WC should be on the left because that is what will be used to tie the LHK on the HC.
2. A half of the Vertical LHK should be made to move using the WC over or under (as the case may be) the HC to have a counterclockwise loop. Gradually pulling it left, you should make it go over the WC to get the crossing point. Once the crossing point is gotten, tie the other half of the Vertical LHK by passing the WC under or over the HC, while pulling it left, pass it under the WC to also make the crossing point.
3. More Vertical LHK should be tied and should be done from the center in the direction of one end. When the first half of the handle is 6 inches, you should stop.
4. The whole sennit or cords should be rotated and back to the center, leaving the WC on the right. Loose ends should be made in clockwise directions as tying of knots is resumed, and once the handle attains a length of 12 inches, you should stop.
5. The four segments should be brought together, thereby folding the sennit. Locate the WC in the process. Tie a SK using the 2 WC, and it should be tight. The fillers are going to be the short cords.
6. Folding the 2 WC means we should have 4 cords to work with. A suitable decorative knot by the user should be used alongside this wonderful design, some of the best knots to use alongside it are; the Square Knot, the Vertical larks head, and the Half hitches with

holding cords. A minimum of six inches of material should be attached to the hook at the end of the pet leach.

7. To attach the hook, two cords should be passed through the loop that is on the hook, and a tight finishing should be tied with the four cords. The glue should be used here as the four cords are being tightened. When it gets dry, all additional materials should be removed or cut to make the work very neat and beautiful. You may also consider another finishing style, which entails that you move the ends in the direction of the strap and put it under the back of the knots so that it can be very tight.

Hammock Chair

Materials to Be Used

- Fabric glue
- Measuring tape
- Two 3-inch heavy-duty metal rings
- 6mm of cord material

Knots to Be Used

- Larks Head Knots (LHK)
- Wrapped Knot (WK)
- Overhand Knot (OK)
- Double Half Hitch (DHH)
- Alternative Square Knot (ASK)
- Barrel Knot (BK)

Steps

1. Let eight 4.5-yard cords pass through one of the rings and balance it by matching the ends. Let the cords be folded at the lower side of the ring. Another eight 3.5-yard cords should be put on the top and should be folded and balanced. A WK should be tied around the cords by placing in the right of the cords that were folded beside the ring, one end of a 50-inch cord. Fold the cord after moving it 2 inches down with the working end taken to the place close to the ring.

2. This working end should be wrapped around the cords, and also the end of the WC secured and wrapped firmly while moving forward till you're almost at the fold. This folded part should look like a loop, and the working end should be passed through it. The secured end of the knot at the top should be pulled, which in turn will pull the working end and the loop in the WK. Both ends of the cord flush should be trimmed with the top and bottom of the WK, and the stubs tucked where they are invisible.

3. Step 1 should be repeated with the other 3.5, and the 4.5-yard cords should be mounted to the other ring in the same way. Each cord should be carefully pulled so that the ring can be tightly clutched without gliding on the ring.

4. The rings should be placed on the work surface or hung up. 2 very short cords from the right ring and from the left should be selected and also lie close to the other coming out

from the WK. These cords are going to be the holding cords for the upper region of the design. The cords should be diagonally placed to meet at a point.

5. The left cords should be numbered 1, 2 while the right 3, 4. They should be used to tie an SK with 1 and 4 as the WCs while 2, 3 are fillers. The cords for the back and seat will be mounted on both sides of the knot.

6. The ends of the 4 cords should be moved to the right and left lying beside the part coming from the rings. Mount the cords of the back and seat on all 4 parts; this can best be mounted using a flat table for horizontal positioning.

7. A 7-yard cord should be folded in half and laid towards you on the 4 holding cords left of the SK. The halves should be put under the holding cords and towards you over the folded area, more like the reverse of an LHK. Some rooms should be left between the Knot and the SK on the holding cord. From the right half of the cord, a half hitch should be tied putting it right of the LHK. It should be passed over and under the holding cord pulling it towards your direction and tightened firmly. The other half of the WC should make a half hitch to the left of the LHK and tighten firmly.

8. The first WC should be placed by the right, so it lies against the SK. This process should be repeated for the other 7-yard cords making a total of 16 cords placed on both sides of the SK in the middle of the HC. Accuracy in measurement is highly important at this stage, as well as the number of rows, so the spaces are correctly matched with the number of side supports.

9. 21 rows of ASK should be tied as we make the back of this design. The first row must rest against the knots used in step 5, and the others should be an inch apart or ¾ inches depending on your size choice. Tie the left SK in row 1 with cords 1–32 and 33–64 with the right. This should be repeated for the odd-numbered rows. The left SK in row 2 should be tied with cords 3–34 and 35–62 with the right, repeating this for even-numbered rows.

10. The knots in row 22 should be well-tightened and lying half-inch below row 21 as we start the seats. This should be done for the other rows. For a tighter wave, the knots can

be arranged ¼ inch apart, but the panel must stretch sideways, and the knots shouldn't be tied close to each other, so the panels don't become too narrow. The process should stop after tying 23 rows.

11. The rings should be used to hand the Hammock chair and two of the long side supports from the right and left each should be selected, and the four selected cords should be diagonally moved facing each other as was done in step 3. Down the WK, about 60 inches should be measured, and it is at this point that the cords should come together. The SK should be tied to connect them together for a while, it is expedient to put the seat on the HC to verify how deep the Hammock chair is because the seats should come up for it to be on an angle to the back but it mustn't be too high, otherwise it won't be comfortable. The place where the HC is tied should be changed so that the seat can go up or down.

12. After the lower HC is rightly placed, the SK should be well tied as glue is applied

13. The ends of the new HC should be moved so that two of them go to the right and the other two to the left with DHH. The only difference between this step and step 5 is the type of knot used. Moving from the center to the outside, you should attach the cords on either side of the SK. A BK should be tied with the cords so that the knots can lie under the seat of the design beside to the lower edge. The seat can either be done by passing the ends via the loops behind the seat, then trimmed a little (the minimum length should be 2 inches though) and glued to hold them together. The seat can also be done by trimming the cords with a fringe left for them to dangle. BK should be tied at the tips to avoid unraveling.

14. The other cords should be organized in pairs for the right-side support. Moving from the top to the bottom, you should attach them to the right of the back and the seat. The SK in row 42 should be next to the first side support, which is 2 rows above the bottom BHH. One of the long side supports (4.5 yards) should slide through a space next to the SK, and the same must be done with the second in a separate space next to the same SK. The side support must be straight and with minimal tension. Both cords should be tied with OK

and tightened firmly for it to touch the back of the seat. Another OK should be tied near the first, and it must rest next to the Hammock chair after tightening. Before moving on, the ends of the front of the seat should be pulled.

15. Step 11 should be repeated with the last long side supports, putting them after every third row along the right of the sat. This should be repeated with the short side supports while working in the upper area that the rows of the SK are far apart. The space should also be every three rows and ensure that the supports are put very close to the SK even while the spaces are very large. Placing the support cords into the position below the whole right side and holding them with knots is very helpful as it can help you adjust the placement accordingly.

16. Steps 11 and 12 should be repeated while attaching the left side support. There should be adjustments made to the knots if needed for the Hammock chair to hang steadily.

17. From where you began, pass the end of the side support through some other more appropriate space further into the left. They should be tied together with 2 OK just like step 11. Another side supports should also go through this step on both sides. The glue should be applied to the knots after finishing and allowed to dry.

Macramé Wall Hanging

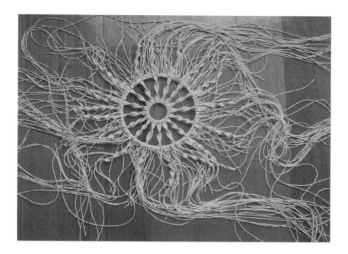

Materials to Be Used

- Macramé Rope – 4mm rope – cords (twelve) 12 – 16″ (as in feet) will be needed. Note this is a long hanging wall, which is why we need longer cords.
- 1 shorter piece of cord to act as your hanger. Only tie it with a simple knot on either end there.
- A dowel or string.

Steps

1. Tie some cord around the end of your dowel. This will be the hanger for our project. Having a Macramé wall hanging while standing is much better than sitting flat.
2. Start by folding the 16′ cords in half. Verify that the ends are even.
3. Place the cord loop under your dowel and thread through the loop the ends of the rope. Tight drive. That's your first reverse Lark's head knot. (For assistance see simple Macramé knots.)
4. Repeat step 3 with 11 cords left over.
5. Allow the first 2 rows of Square Knots. (For assistance see simple Macramé knots.)
6. Render now 2 rows of Alternating Square Knots.
7. Now make another 2 rows of knots in Square.

8. Follow this pattern (2 rows of square knots, 2 rows of alternating square knots) until you have 10 rows in all.

9. Working from left to right, make double half-hitch knots around your piece in a diagonal pattern.

10. Create 2 more square-knots lines. We will finish the hanging wall with a set of spiral knots, which is essentially just a sequence of half-square knots (or left side square knots). (Do not complete the right side of the square knot, only consistently make the left side square knots, and it will spiral to you.)

Macramé Pillow

Materials to Be Used

- Macramé Cord Scissors Sewing Machine / Thread (optional)
- Pillow cover and attach Dowel or Stick Tape Measure to this pillow, you can either start with a pillow cover that you already have or make a simple pillow cover. But don't just make it yet, see first Stage 5.

Steps

1. Cut the cords in! To make this pattern, you'll need 16–12-foot cords.
2. Use reverse lark's head knots to tie 16 of your cords to your dowel.
3. The pattern for this cover is just 1 alternating square knot in the line. Leave a little gap between each knot, around half an inch as a reference point. What's more, having a bit of space makes the project go much faster.

4. Create two horizontal rows of (left-to-right, then right-to-left) or double half-hitch knots until you touch down.

5. Now that we're done with the pattern, cut off the excess from the bottom but keep a little fringe.

6. Now you're either going to remove your dowel or simply cut it off at Step 5, how can you add this to your pillow cover?

7. Here's how to attach your Macramé pattern to your pillow. Before you sew it up, if you're making a cover yourself, you're essentially going to line up the pattern to the front of your cover, leaving the cut ends a little over the top hang.

8. Lay down the pattern over the front and put the back piece on top!

9. Place the back piece over your cover and Macramé template—right sides facing each other—essentially you make a sandwich here, and the Macramé is called the "meat."

10. Now just patch your pillow cover's top seam—go over the ropes too! It takes some degree of finesse, but you can.

11. Shove the Macramé pattern within your pillow to stitch the rest of your cover, and stitch the remaining seams as usual.

12. Flip it straight out. Now you should have your Macramé pattern added to the top of your pillow (coming out from inside between the seams).

13. Take and loop a cord through your pattern.

14. Take the other hand through your pillow on the bottom. Do this many times (crisscross) and knot it!

15. And it is! It's left your fringe dangling from the edges.

16. Even if the pillow cover is ready-made.

Mirror Wall Hanging

Materials to Be Used

- Macramé Cording: 4mm
- Mirrored octagon
- 2 inches Wood ring
- Wood beads: 25mm w/10mm hole size
- Strong scissors

Steps

1. Cut 4 pieces of cording Macramé into sections of 108 inches (or 3 yds.). Cut the strips in half and tie all of them with a Lark's Head knot on the wood loop. Tightly and closely pull the knots. Separate two head knots from the Lark and begin to tie them into a square knot. Start tying into the second two Lark's Head knots two square knots. As you start the

second knot of the square, loop it through one of the sides of the other two knots into a wide knot of the square. Fasten 7 square knots on both sides. Break the ends after the knots have been tied. Two strings per side and four in the center. To secure the frayed ends, apply tape to the ends of the thread. This will make inserting the beads simpler. Congratulations. That's been the toughest part! The others are easy ties to tie and even get the sides.

2. In each of the 2 side cording lines, apply one bead. Tie a knot on both sides under the bead to keep them even. Connect the four cords in the middle to a simple or (overhand knot) about 1/14 inch below the beads. Take a cord from the center and add it to the sides of the two cords. Tie the three on both sides in a knot. Apply the mirror to the end of the knot. Add one of the three sides to the mirror's back to hold it steady. Place clear knots in all 3 side cables at the bottom left and right side of the mirror. Trim the cords again on all three sides. Return one to the back of the mirror on either side and add two to the front of it on each side.

3. Flip the mirror over and tie together all the cords. Flip over the mirror and loosen the knot at the front. Inside the knot, slip the back cords and straighten the knot. Cutting the cord ends up to around 14 inches. Take the ends or loose the cord and let them break. Combine the ends of the cording to fluff ends with a comb. Hang up and have fun!

Toilet Paper Holders

Materials to Be Used

- 11 cords of 13 inches each
- Scissors
- Tape measure
- Macramé board

Steps

1. Get 9 cords, divide it into 3, to have 3 cords on each side; braid the cords together.
2. Get 1 cord from the 2 remaining ones: place it at one end of the braid. Make a loop with it and carefully and neatly tie it to that end, so it will have an aesthetic look.
3. Do the same with the other cord at the other end and you will have a new holder for your tissue paper. Not just any holder, but a Macramé holder!

Macramé Mason Jars

Materials to Be Used

- Macramé Cord
- Mason Jars
- Scissors
- Macramé Wood Rings

Steps

1. On both jars, cut the cords at the same lengths—at the end, you'll have to cut off the excess on the regular-sized jar. Still, having too much cord is better than getting too little!

2. Creating a Macramé Mason jar, the larger Mason jar has a pattern of one alternating square knot all the way around. For each jar, your cording will be 6 feet long.

3. For the larger jar, you'll need 6 cords, and the smaller jar will require 8 cords.

4. Standard Mason jar (known in this tutorial as Standard): the pattern is 2 square knots followed by 2 alternating square knots all the way around.

5. To begin each jar: take 2 of your 6-ft. ropes and fold them over the container's lip—secure them with a solitary square knot. Bigger: take 1 of your 6-ft. lines and fold them over the container's lip—with a standard knot tight.

6. Start with the head knots of the lark. Proceed with the Lark's head knots.

7. Join the remaining lines. Regular: take the remainder of your 6 ropes and bind them to your container utilizing the reverse Lark's head knots. Bigger: take the rest of your 5 strings and affix them to your container utilizing the reverse Lark's head knots. The knots space are consistently around the container's edge.

8. Making scattered square knots produce square knots 3 scattered. Tie square knots. Regular: make 2 knots in the square right around. Bigger: make a 1-column exchanging square knot around the container as far as possible. Continue the pattern down the jar: make a row of 2 alternating square knots now normal. Continue on these alternating rows of square knots until you reach the bottom of the pot. Larger: Start along the way with another series of alternating square knots. Repeat so until it hits the jar's rim.

9. Alternating Mason jar square knots Hint: have you got a handle on your pot? Getting the knots around or around the handle just fits around it.

10. Creating fringe Macramé 5 on the bottom of the Mason jar. Finish the bottle. Regular / Larger: cut off any excess rope before you get to the bottom of the jar, but leave it a little there and comb it out for a fringe look.

11. However, if you really wanted to cover the whole pot, you might use smaller sized rope and make alternating square knots very tightly weaved.

Dragonfly

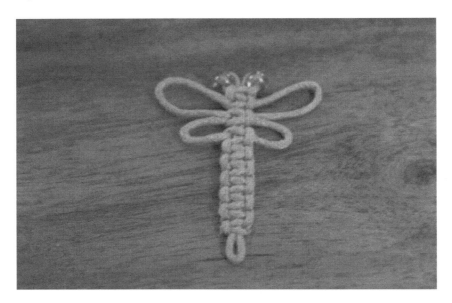

Materials to Be Used

- Cord material of between 2 and 4 millimeter in length
- Half a dozen roller beads or more
- Pins and boards for the project
- Dry clear glue for fabric

Steps

1. Cut 1 cord of 72 inches or 2 yards in length. Use glue to prepare the ends and let it completely dry. The dragonfly's head is created with a single bead. With the cords held by your two hands, create a loop and cross the end on the left over that of the right. From below bring the left end through the loop. Tighten and push the tips into the beads, one after the other.

2. Keep the Satin Dragonfly's (SD) head secure by moving the pin through the gap that the OK created. Using the cord's left half, create a counterclockwise loop.

3. Finish the OK by shifting the left end through the loop below and then over (from below). Do not make the knot tight.

4. Through the knot you just made, push the cord's right half through, and rotate in the clockwise direction as it passes over and then under the loop. Draw to the right and then push it over the cord that was worked on, that is, the half that is on the right.

5. Finish the OK on the right by pushing the tip into the loop, first under and then over (from below). Position the 2 knots so that both the inner portions and the outer portions can be seen clearly. Put them near bead, and apart with plenty space. It is important to note that the crook or the rounded area is the inner part of both knots. The left knot's inner part should be held and moved rightward. Move it through the right knot's outer crossed part. It should also be passed beneath the segment that leads to the SD's top, and on top of the segment that leads to the end. Bring the right knot's inner part to the left knot's crossed area. Move it the same way that is below the top segment, and above the part that leads to the end. Make the wings of the SD tight, and move it as close to the bead as you can. Possibly, reposition the knot and eliminate the slack that is on top of the knot. With the ends steady, draw on the loops first. Then with the center tightened, shorten the loops by pulling on the tips. They should have an approximate length on one inch. Repeat the 2nd to 7th step more than once to create extra sets of wings and try to put them closely.

6. Behind the hanger knot, add glue and let it dry. Join a bead to the two cords as was done with the first one at the top of the SD. Make an OK with both ends working together. Repeat the 8th step multiple times, till you get the desired tail size. Glue the final knot tied both on the outside and on the inside.

Mini Pumpkin Macramé Hanger

Materials to Be Used

- Black thread or line
- Metal loop
- Hollow pearls
- Scissors

Steps

1. Cut 4 yarn strands about 3 times the completed hanger length. Fold the threads in the middle of the metal hoop.
2. The yarn strands are then divided into two groups.
3. Connect a knot to each group.
4. Cord a wooden bead on each thread, then tie another knot just below the bead.
5. Join a pair of knots a couple of inches apart.
6. Then tie two neighboring strings together and repeat each string. Then tie with the first line the last line.
7. Continue this process and bring another string together.
8. Finally, tie all the strings in a large knot.

Macramé Wreath Project

Materials to Be Used

- 10 "Alloy Silver Ring
- 27 '100% Graphite Cotton Rope – 5 mm
- Scissors
- Glue Gun
- Banding (optional)

Steps

1. We used Benzie felt shades in Oats, Rosewood, Strawberry, and Sage, as well as large medium and tiny poms in Graphite, Orchid, and Blush for producing the pots.

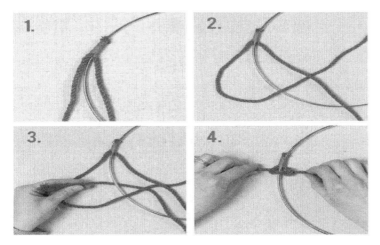

2. Image 1: Tie two ends of the rope to the ring (you'll want two lengths identical to each other). Another beginning method (not seen here) is to take the complete length of the rope (not reduced to two different lengths), locate the center and place it around the ring at one point until it is halved and two identical lengths of rope are on each side of the ring, then make a basic knot around the loop.

3. Image 2: Make a backward D formation with the left rope and carry the rope over the top of the ring and under the right rope.

4. Image 3: Take the rope from the right side of the ring and move it through the pipe, through the D-shaped rear opening and over the top of the rope to the west.

5. Image 4: Tighten all rope lengths to shape the Half Knot.

6. Does the same Half Knot (photo measures 2–4) across the metal ring over and over again. The ties curl around the ring to create a beautiful pattern. Cut the rope ends as the whole ring is full of knots leaving only enough space to firmly tie the ends onto the knots on the back of the wreath. To do this, we consider using a hot glue piston.

7. Arrange the completed seeds and then hot glue them.

Macramé Shelf Project

Materials to Be Used

- Square 2-inch diameter Macramé shelf with double handhold cutouts
- Yellow cotton fleece
- Clippers

Steps

1. Place a triangular Macramé shelf 2 feet in diameter on a flat surface with double handhold cutouts.

2. Cut 2 yellow yarn pieces lengthwise to 8 feet. Fold the yarn in half and cut each section in the middle to make 4 individual pieces of yarn.

3. Lay the 4 yarn threads out lengthwise and ensure that the sides are uniformly lined up.

4. Drag the ends of the yarn through the handhold cutouts at the bottom corner of the rack.

5. Fold 6 inches of the yarn ends in half to build a loop and draw the remaining yarn ends to construct a knot through the thread. Zoom in to close.

6. By using 2 center layers of yellow yarn as a base, lay the strand in a backward L-shape from the right side of the group across the top of the center.

7. Loop the strand below the two center strands from the left side and up and between the rear L-shape and the farthest strand on the right. To build a stylish Macramé knot, tap tightly.

8. Repeat the process to create a second knot, directly below the first knot. Push the first knot up to meet the second.

9. Continue to design Macramé knots until six are in rows.

10. Use 4 additional yellow yarn strands to repeat the process on top of the same cutout with the same handhold.

11. Gather the excess yarn at the ends of both knotted Macramé strings and thread into one knot.

12. Replicate the entire process on the other side of the circular shelf for the handholding cutout.

13. Hang the shelf on either side from the 2 top knots, so the shelf is horizontal to the ground.

14. Place a vine, paper, or candle onto the show Macramé table.

Lantern Bracelet

Materials to Be Used

- 3 strands of C-Lon cord (2 light brown and 1 medium brown) 63-inch lengths
- Fasteners (1 jump ring, 1 spring ring or lobster clasp)
- Glue – Beacon 527 multi-use
- 8 small beads (about 4 mm) amber to gold colors
- 30 gold seed beads
- 3 beads (about 6 mm) amber color (mine are rectangular, but round or oval will work wonderfully too)

Note: Bead size can vary slightly. Just be sure all beads you choose will slide onto 2 cords (except seed beads).

Knots to Be Used

- Lark's Head Knot
- Spiral Knot
- Picot Knot
- Overhand Knot

Steps

1. Find the center of your cord and attach it to the jump ring with a Lark's head knot. Repeat with the 2 remaining strands. If you want the 2-tone effect, be sure your second color is not placed in the center, or it will only be a filler cord and you will end up with a 1-tone bracelet.

2. You now have 6 cords to work with. Think of them as numbered 1 thorough 6, from left to right. Move cords 1 and 6 apart from the rest. You will use these to work the spiral knot. All others are filler cords. Take cord number 1 and tie a spiral knot. Always begin with the left cord. Tie 7 more spirals.

3. Place a 4mm bead on the center 2 cords. Leave cords 1 and 6 alone for now and work 1 flat knot using cords 2 and 5.

4. Now put cords 2 and 5 together with the center strands. Use cords 1 and 6 to tie a picot flat knot. If you don't like the look of your picot knot, loosen it up and try again. Gently tug the cords into place and then lock in tightly with the spiral knot.
   Notice here how I am holding the picot knot with my thumbs while pulling the cords tight with my fingers. If you look closely, you may be able to see that I have a cord in each hand.

5. Tie 8 spiral knots (using the left cord throughout the pattern).

6. Place a 4mm bead on the center 2 cords. Leave cords 1 and 6 alone for now and work 1 flat knot using cords 2 and 5. Now put cords 2 and 5 together with the center strands. Use strands 1 and 6 to tie a picot flat knot.

7. Repeat steps 5 and 6 until you have 5 sets of spirals.

8. Place 5 seed beads on cords 1 and 6. Put cords 3 and 4 together and string on a 6mm bead. Tie one flat knot with the outermost cords.

9. Repeat this step two more times.

10. Now repeat steps 5 and 6 until you have 5 sets of spirals from the center point. Thread on your clasp. Tie an overhand knot with each cord and glue well. Let it dry completely.

As this is the weakest point in the design, I advise trimming the excess cords and gluing them again. Let it dry.

Double Coin Knot Cuff

Materials to Be Used

- 9 m (10 yds.) 2mm leather cord
- 3 x 9mm internal dimension end caps magnetic fastening

Steps

1. Cut the leather cord into three equal pieces, 3 m (31/3 yd.) long. Referring to Chinese Knots: Double Coin Knot, tie a double coin knot using all three strands starting in your left hand with a clockwise loop and pulling down the working end (right-hand tail) over the thread. Complete the knot and make it tight so that the top loop is relatively wide and all three strands are smooth and neatly aligned.
2. Make a second double coin knot, this time starting with a loop in your right hand, bringing the working end (left-hand tail) down through the loop, around the other tail, and doubling back to create the second knot.
3. Firm the second knot, adjust the position so that the previous knot is fairly close but does not overlap. Make sure none of the cords are twisted and that they all lie flat inside the knot.

4. Continue to tie double coin knots one by one and swap the starting position from side to side each time.

5. Analyze the length of the cuff until you've made six knots. If required, adjust the distance between each knot to allow for the fastening.

6. Overlap the cords after the final knot to create a circle. Either tie the cords together or stitch them across to hold the cord flat, depending on the style of your end cap (see Finishing Techniques). Trim the ends and use epoxy resin glue to hold into the end caps.

Prosperity Knot Belt

Materials to Be Used

- 8.5 m (9 yds.) 2mm wax cotton cord

- 12mm (1/2 in.) long buckle

- Small piece of leather

- E6000 jewelry glue

Steps

1. Fold the cord in half to locate the center and tie a double coin knot in the middle, beginning with a loop on the left side. Referring to Chinese Knots: Prosperity Knot, a somewhat loose knot of prosperity tends to tie in. Firm by raising all of the overlapping cords up, one at a time, to the top of the knot, until two loops are left at the bottom.

2. Pull through the top left cord to pull one side of the bottom loop up. Repeat on the other side. Then pull the tails one by one to get the knot tight.

3. Repeat the firming up the process if necessary, to create a 12mm (1/2 in.) wide, closely woven prosperity knot. Hold the knot tightly in two hands between fingers and thumbs and agitate gently to align the cords in a pattern that is even more woven.

4. Tie a double coin knot to the tails, this time starting with a loop on the right side. If the knot is tied, change the location, so it is similar to the knot of success but does not overlap it. Carefully set up because you won't be able to change it later.

5. Continue to tie alternative stability and double knots of coinage.

6. Remember to alternate the side on which the start loop is an on-left loop for the knot of prosperity and the right loop for the knot of the double coin.

7. Stop after tying a prosperity knot once the belt has the appropriate length allowing for overlap. Loop the ends twice on either side around the belt buckle to fill the void, and stitch tightly backward.

8. Cut a 1 x 3 cm (1/8 x 11/8 in.) leather strap to create the belt loop.

9. Apply glue to one end of the leather strip and hold below the buckle over the stitched cord ends. Loop the strap around the belt, so it overlaps on the opposite side, leaving a loop wide enough to pass through the other end of the belt. Apply glue to the overlapping strip and stay until the adhesive seals. Leave before use, for 24 hours.

DIY Dream catcher

Materials to Be Used

- Twine
- 420mm Ring
- 175mm Ring
- 40mm Ring

Steps

1. Using a 40mm loop, with a Lark's head knot tie the twine into the circle and then use half tie twist to build the spiral know-how function. Spiral out before the next 175mm ring is fit for connecting. Further twine is then larks heading all the way around on the 175mm ring (making it seem like a magnificent sea creature), there are plenty of twines to dispute at this stage! The final ring of 420 mm is connected, so several severe Macramé knots will now occur.

Laptop Mat

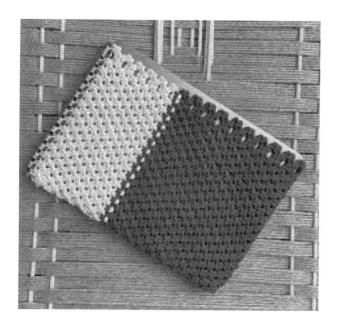

Materials to Be Used

- Wooden board
- 4–5 clips
- Scissors
- Measuring tape

Knots to Be Used

- Square Knot
- Diagonal double and horizontal double half hitch

Steps

1. Measure 48 bits of 3 m yarn and split. Leaving around 10 cm of thread, the yarns are tied to a wooden board using 4–5 clips to begin knotting. Tie 12 knots in line, from left to right. Cross out the first two lines. Build a square knot with two strands of the first square knot,

and two strands of the first row's second square knot. Continue to tie 10 more knots in square to have eleven knots in a series. Create rows of square ties, missing the first. Two strands for the fourth, sixth, eighth, and tenth sets. Full one side with double half-hitch horizontal. Skip three threads and the next five knots in the line. Avoid five threads and the following four knots in the front. Ignore the next three square ties and the seven ribbons. Miss the next two square ties and the nine threads. Avoid the eleven threads and one square knot then.

2. Move to 12th row: Use the 3rd strand as the keeping rope, attach ten double half hitch diagonally downwards from left to right. Using the 24th strand as the keeping string, attach ten double half hitch diagonally downwards from right to left. Skip the 25th strand and tie the next 5 knots in the line. Avoid the 25th–27th strand and tie the next four ties. Miss the 25th–29th strand and tie the next three knots. Miss the 25th–31st strand and tie the next two knots. Remove the 25th–33rd strand and tie the next one knot. Link 10 double half hook from left to right diagonally down using the 25th strand as holding the thread. Using the 46th strand as the keeping string, attach 10 double half hitches diagonally downwards from right to left. Tie the square knots to build a thirteen to twenty-one row diamond pattern. Try to tie the design with square knots and a double half hook diagonally until you get the template. Full a double half-hitch horizontal. Line 34 to 43: make rows of square knots, missing the first 2 lines for row 34, 36, 38, 40, and 42. Split the two ends smooth and even to the desired length.

Macramé Table linen

Materials to Be Used

- Swivel Hook
- Glue
- Board and pins
- Buttonhole Clasp
- Linen

Knots to Be Used

- Square Knots (SK)
- Overhand Knot

Steps

1. Put the two cords vertically on our board after getting their corresponding midpoints and tightly place them close to each other. The longer should be on the left because that is what will be used to tie the HC. Half of the Vertical LHK should make to move using the WC over or under (as the case may be), they have a counterclockwise loop. Gradually,

pulling it to the left, you should make it go over so that they get the crossing point. Once the crossing point is gotten, tie the other Half of the Vertical LHK by passing the WC under or over the HC, while pulling it left, pass it under the WC as well to make the crossing point. More Vertical LHK should be tied and should be done from the center in the direction of one end. When the first half of the handle is 6 inches, you should stop. The whole sennit or cords should be rotated and back to the center, leaving the WC on the right. Loose ends should be made in clockwise directions as tying of knots is resumed, and once the handle attains a length of 12 inches, you should stop, the four segments should be brought together, thereby folding the sennit. Locate the WC in the process. Tie a SK using the 2 WC, and it should be tight. The fillers are going to be the short cords folding the 2 WC, which means we should have 4 cords to work with. A suitable decorative knot by the user should use alongside this wonderful design; some of the best knots to use alongside it are; the Square Knot, the Vertical Lark's head, and the Half hitch with holding cords. A minimum of six inches of material should be attached to the hook at the end of the pet leach. To attach the hook, two cords should pass through the loop that is on the hook. Tight finishing should be tied with the four cords. The glue usage comes in here as the four cords are being tighten, the glue should be used. When it gets dry, all additional materials should be removed or cut to make the work very neat and beautiful. You may also consider another finishing style, which entails that you move the ends in the direction of the strap and put it under the back of the knots to be very firm.

A Macramé Bracelet

If different knots are combined to realize a single complex or motif, Macramé designs can be made. The following could be used to produce a Macramé strap:

Materials to Be Used

- Scissors or razor blade
- A crayon or T-pin or foam frame
- A hemp cord or a string of choice

Steps

1. The width of the wrist is first calculated. Then cut two bits of hemp cord with the aid of the scissors. The cut pieces will be at least three times the length of the wrist or even the diameter initially measured. For example, if the measurement is 5 inches, two strands of 15 inches should be cut.

2. One strand is partially folded. When the handle is kept in a horizontal position, the folding strand is protected with a loop over the pencil, which ensures that loose ends are placed behind it. Those loose ends should be tightly pulled and crossed by the loop.

3. This cycle should also be replicated in the second strand. You'll finally have to hang this pencil down with four lines. Mentally, you can mark 4 strands as 1, 2, 3, and 4 from right to left. Any labeling technique you find simple can be used.

4. Therefore, beach 1 will be moved to the west over beach 2 and beach 3 (which are the two main beaches) and then below beach 4.

5. Take strand 4 at this step behind both strands 2 and 3 through the loop created by strand 1. Pull strand 1 and strand 4 tightly to ensure a half-square knot is achieved.

6. You can now conduct a crossing process. Continue this crossing until the bracelet eventually reaches your desired duration. Spirals will be formed as the half-square knots start to operate.

7. The loops have gone out of the crayon here. Pull strand 2 and strand 3 to marginally develop the loop size. Instead, the four threads are tied together, and the job is secured by two knots. Those are main knots. Those strings that you assume are unwanted should be cut off and reached as close to those knots as possible.

8. Now you put your watch on your wrist. To hold the bracelet on your handle, move the knot through the loop.

9. The steps above will allow you to design a simple Macramé bracelet. This approach to Macramé uses knotting rather than weaving or knitting. You can also make a beaded necklace with Macramé beads. The Macramé approach helps you to design various bracelet styles. This is up to you.

Macramé Camera Strap

Materials to Be Used

- Macramé Loop
- Four fasteners
- Clothing spinner
- Industrial adhesive resistance
- Scissors

Steps

Step 1: Cut 2 lengths of the Macramé thread, each 4 yards.

Step 2: Fold each cord length to make 1 yard on one side and 3 yards on the other. Attach the intermediate points by the flap of a swivel clasp that holds the long ends of the external strands.

Step 3: Tie each cord by its own loop and safe it around the clasp.

Step 4: Start tying a square knot. Take the left (longest) cord, cross it over the middle and the bottom of two cords (longest one). Then bring up and down the right cord below the middle of the two and the left cord. Pull this taut. It is half the square knot.

Step 5: Complete the reverse move 4 square knot. Cross in the middle of two the right chord, then the left chord in the middle of two, then the right one. Pull close and finish the square with a knot.

Step 6: Continue to tie square knots to the appropriate camera strap length.

Step 7: Trim all four ends of the thread. Join all four cords through another pivoting bond. At the bottom of each thread, fold the cords over the clasp and hold clothespins until the adhesive dries.

Remove the clips and pop the strap when the glue is hot on your frame! I love a camera strap with a Macramé cord because it's very light and flexible around your neck.

Knotted Chevron Headband

Materials to Be Used

- Broder floss (6 colors/12 suits my 1/2-inch-wide headband)
- The satin narrow belt – 1/8 to 1/4" is perfect
- E6000 or equivalent adhesive plastic
- 1/2 centimeter long or your favorite headband
- Matched thread and needle sewing (preferably if you want to place the knotted part on the headband for extra stability)

Steps

1. Start by making your extra-long friendship bracelet.
2. I've been using 6 strands each 10 feet in length, half by 5 feet, but if your head band is wider, maybe your headband would be bigger.

3. Hold a removable knot together and tie the strands and operate the Classic Chevron Friendship Bracelet (or pattern for you) until the strip is 1 to 5 inches longer than the length of the headband.

4. Untie the knot upon completion.

5. Put a dot of glue on the back of your headband and put it around your headband. Make sure you cover the band on the front and back and if you have a single face on the satin belt, the good side is off.

6. Cut off the tails one end of the knitted strip and hold it down. Save it for a few minutes.

7. Put some glue on your back and tie the knotted strip to the rope until it is imperfect.

8. So go on gluing and binding, but then behind the knotted thread.

9. Avoid gluing and wrapping when the knotted strip is as far away from the other end.

10. Cut the tails to the end and add the whole length of the super long bracelet to the end. Likely, you will extend it a little to match and that's perfect. (Keep it to the end only if you want to stitch the kneaded part on the back.)

11. Hold on the end of the strip and tie it smoothly on your back to the end of the headband.

12. When you just hang up, you can thread the knotted piece back and forth on the edges and draw it close. This is a good choice because the line has very straight edges.

Macramé DIY Guitar Strap

Materials to Be Used

- Macramé cord
- Active Clasps
- Nice areas
- Industrial resistance to adhesive
- Scissors

Steps

Step 1: Cut 2 Macramé cord lengths, every 4 yards.

Step2: Fold the length of each string so that one yard is on one side and three yards on the other side. Insert the centers on the thread outside, which leave the long ends, in the flat part of the swivel handle.

Step 3: Push each cord into its own circuit and close its knot.

Step 4: Begin making a square knot. Take the longest left string and cross the middle of each string and underneath the left string. Take the right cord under the center two and the left cord up and down. Pull this taut. That's half your knot square.

Step 5: Complete the square knot with reverse step 4. Intersect the right cord over the center two and the bottom left; then, under the center two, across the center and over the left cord. A quick pull and a square knot was completed.

Step 6: Keep adding your square knots for your guitar strap to the right length.

Step 7: Trim all four ends of the thread. In a pivoting knot, join all four cords. At the end of each string, put a dollop of adhesive, fold the strings and hold clothespins until the adhesive is soft.

Replace the clips until the glue is dry and pop your strap!

Macramé Bathmat

Materials to Be Used

- 3 bundles of strong and hard cords, as the texture of jute
- Scissors
- Matching color of thread and needle
- A Macramé board

Steps

1. With the three bundles of cords, form a tight loop.
2. From the loop, make the second, third, and fourth loop.
3. Continue looping and get the rope to be as long as possible. Make enough loops that will suffice for the whole mat.
4. When any one of the cords is about to finish, cut it off and continue with the looping; until you have one cord remaining.
5. Tie the end of this cord very well, so that it will not loosen.

6. Go to the beginning of the cords and cut off the strands there.

7. Fold it to have a length of about eight inches.

8. Use the needle and thread to stitch where the fold was made. Continue with the stitching until you get to the end of the fold. Fold the braided cords over and continue with the stitching.

9. While maintaining a flat work, do this over and over, until you get to the end of the braided cords.

10. At that point, stitch and tighten it securely, so that it will not loosen. Your bathmat is ready to be used.

Celtic Choker

Elegant loops allow the emerald and silver beads to stand out, making this a striking piece. The finished length is 12 inches. Be sure to use the ribbon clasp which gives you multiple length options to the closure.

Alternating Lark's Head Chain

- 3 strands of black C-Lon cord; two 7-ft. cords, one 4-ft. cord
- 18 – green beads (4 mm)
- 7 – round silver beads (10 mm)
- Fasteners: Ribbon Clasps, silver

Note: Bead size can vary slightly. Just make sure all the beads you choose will slide onto 2 cords.

Steps

1. Optional – Find the center of your cord and attach it to the top of the ribbon clasp with a knot. I found it easier to thread the loose ends through and pull them down until my loop was near the opening, then push the cords through the loop. Repeat with the 2 remaining strands, putting the 4-foot cord in the center. If this is problematic, you could cut all the

93

cords to 7-ft. and not worry about placement. (If you really trust your glue, you can skip this step by gluing the cords into the clasp and going from there.)

2. Lay all cords into the ribbon clasp. Add a generous dap of glue and use pliers to close the clasp.

3. You now have 6 cords to work with. Find the 4-ft. cords and place them in the center. They will be the holding (or filler) cords throughout.

4. Begin your Alternating Lark's Head (ALH) chain, using the outmost right cord and then the outermost left cord. Follow with the other right cord and then the last left cord. For this first set, the pattern will be hard to see. You may need to tug gently on the cords to get a little slack in them.

5. Now slide a silver bead onto the center 2 cords.

6. The outer cords are now staggered on your holding cords. Continue with the ALH chain by knotting with the upper right cord and then tie a knot with the upper left cord.

7. Finish your set of 4 knots, then add a green bead.

8. Tie four ALH knots followed by a green bead until you have 3 green beads in the pattern. Then tie one more set of 4 ALH knots.

9. Slide on a silver bead and continue creating sequences of 3 green, 1 silver (always with 4 ALH knots between each). End with the 7th silver bead and 1 more set of 4 ALH knots, for a 12" necklace.

10. Lay all cords in the ribbon clasp and glue well.

11. Crimp shut and let it dry completely. Trim excess cords.

Climbing Vine Keychain

This pattern is a fun way to practice the Diagonal Double Half-Hitch knot. It works up quickly and is a fun piece to work in various colors. Just be sure to use enough beads on the fringe work to weigh the threads down.

Materials to Be Used

- Measure out 3 cords of Peridot C-Lon, 30" each
- 1 key ring
- 2 (5mm) beads
- 8 (plus extra for ends) pink seed beads
- 4 (plus extra for ends) gold seed beads
- 12 (plus extra for ends) green seed beads
- 8 (plus extra for ends) 3mm pearl beads (seed pearl beads will work also)

Note: You can vary slightly the bead size. Just make sure that 2 cords will fit through the 2 main beads (the 5mm size beads).

Knots to Be Used

- Lark's Head
- Flat Knot
- Diagonal Double Half-Hitch

Steps

1. Fold each cord in half and use to attach it to the key ring. Secure onto your work surface with straight pins. You now have 6 cords to work with.
2. Separate cords into 3 and 3. Using the left 3 cords, tie 2 flat knots. Repeat with the right 3 cords.

Macramé Lamp Wire

Materials to Be Used

- Cords
- Scissors
- Lamp with lamp holder

Steps

1. Measure the length of the cord you want to work on, to determine the length of cord you will use.
2. Cut out your cord and fold it into two.
3. Place it around the cord just before the lamp holder.
4. Take the left side of the cord over to the right and take the right under the cord.
5. Pull the two cords out through the loops.
6. To make it easier for you, fold the left cord over your four fingers to have a big fold. Do the same with the other cord.

7. Take the left one over and the right one under, and pull each side. Do this again and you will notice that the pattern will be twisting.

8. Carry on with the pattern until you get to the end of the cable.

9. For the last knot, make a double half-hitch knot, and cut off the remaining cords with your pair of scissors.

Chapter 5: Advanced Projects

Macramé Headband

We're beginning with a trendy headband to start with. At the beginning of the summer of 2019, we did the idea to wear it at music festivals. We always liked the boho-chic appearance and what better way to build our sense of style than to design a macramé headband of our own.

Fig: Boho-chic headband

In the music event scene, especially among the trendy and stylish, boho-chic fashion culture, these macramé headbands have become very popular. We never ended up going to a music event, but not everything was lost because, over the summer, we ended up wearing it all as it was the ideal piece for any dress.

This project may seem very simple to create to the naked eye, but the complication of this project occurs when you have to make the heart hitch pattern. This is a case where only two knots are used, but the pattern is not easy. The more you learn different ways of using a knot and the patterns to come, the more you can advance your macramé skill set.

It is expected that this project would take about one hour. Time can differ based on skill level and experience. You will need relevant details to get starting on this initiative.

Macramé Materials Needed

- Thread and Needle
- Elastic Headband
- 3mm or 4mm Cotton Cord

Length of Cords

- 1 x 150cm
- 2 x 300cm

If you are into the boho-chic fashion as we are, this is a great start for the intermediate macramé project. We recommend taking your time and then going slow while you are sewing an elastic headband to a pattern to prevent any problems or mishaps. Have fun.

Macramé Necklace

A macramé necklace is the next project design we want to discuss with you. This was another project we designed, which we were expecting to wear if we could have the chance to be at the music festival. We don't usually do the projects like this much, but we were on a boho-style knotting spree and during this particular month.

Fig: Boho-chic sequins necklace

Your emphasis will be on using a smaller diameter cord whether you love DIY fashion shoes, craft jewelry, or making wearable art. The kind of cord that we used was the 1 mm cotton cord for this particular project. Our project has also added sequins and beads and used four knots to form a distinctive style and appearance into the design.

We used the sequins and beads for this project, but you can swap them with any other material that you would choose. You may incorporate buttons, charms, or some other material that makes it its distinctive function.

Don't be scared to go all out and do distinct stuff in most of these projects. You'll soon find your artistic personality and what you love creating.

This project will need the following:

Macramé Supplies Needed

- Sequins
- 1mm Single Strand Cord

Length of Cords

- 6 x 240cm

Macramé Dreamcatcher

A unique form of ancient decoration is dreamcatchers. They are believed to offer supernatural influences derived from Native American culture. To create a net or web-like pattern, they are usually constructed from natural fibers bound together around the wooden hoop. They're meant to possess bearish abilities that fend off bad spirits and preserve your dreams, and that's precisely why we crafted one.

We always have been fascinated by spirituality, and mixing a dream catcher with our passion for macramé was unavoidable. A few months ago, we created this dreamcatcher, and we want to discuss our experience of bringing it all together so that you may have the chance to build your own.

Fig: Dreamcatcher wall hanging

Nowadays, dream catchers, inside and outside, have become a common household decor piece. You will also find them dangling over a baby crib in a nursery or the outside hanging beside the wind chime.

They make for amazing home decor, and we think all macramé designers should strive to make one on their macramé trip at least once.

Macramé Supplies Needed

- Scissors
- Metal Comb
- Measuring Tape
- 3mm Cotton Cord (approximate 35m)
- 19cm Metal ring

Length of Cords

- 8 x 350cm for the rest of a dream catcher
- 1 x 300cm (ring wrap)

It should take around 1–2 hours for the project, but once done, you will have a beautiful dreamcatcher that you can hang over your bed to help you sleep comfortably and shield yourself from any nightmares. Go ahead and give it a shot on this initiative.

Macramé Flower

Aren't flowers gorgeous? For them to attract your eyes, they don't always have to be real.

One of our best activities to do is making flowers to add to our macramé projects. It places a spotlight on what you have made. You will feel that it will enable your project alive by incorporating numerous types of flower styles and leaf/feather patterns.

Fig: Handmade flower with white pearl

We like to add to our wall hanging parts an array of assorted macramé flowers, and we also like to pair them with the other natural macramé-shaped designs, such as feathers or leaves.

We will not consider it to be incredibly challenging for this project. We will place this project between the level of intermediate and advanced skills. We faced this unique project because of the number of knots we had to create using such a thin string to shape the flower pattern. Although it is not a big concern, you will find that on a project like jewelry bracelets, necklace, and macramé flowers identical to this one using smaller diameter cord, you will be expected to spend as much time, if not more time, creating these smaller projects as compared to those of the medium or larger project by using thicker cord such as the macramé plant hanger or a wall hanging. However, learning how to make the macramé flower can dramatically boost your patience, your techniques of binding, and give you lots of practice to expand on your macramé basis.

To start this macramé flower project, you need the following:

Macramé Supplies Needed

- Scissors
- Measuring Tape
- Crochet Needle (optional)
- 1mm cotton cord

Length of Cords

- 1 x 1mm hole beads
- 8 x 200cm length cotton cord (1mm)

To acquire a strong understanding of how to create this pattern, try to make these macramé flowers and give them a try.

Macramé Book or Magazine Holder

Are you the kind of person who loves to get lost in a good book?

For you, this macramé book holder project could be the ideal DIY macramé project if you love reading like us.

Fig: Modern macramé book/magazine holder

We made that project because we decided to add some kind of exclusive home décor to our bathroom; we wanted to hang up something beautifully pleasing and gave the character of the space and a little bit of our touch.

We began this project by binding a wooden dowel with Lark's Head knots. Using two knots, the Clove hitch knot and the Square knot, we then started to design a book/magazine holder to form a special pattern for this project. With the sides fastened together, the bottom portion of the pattern was rolled up, making a wide enough pocket to accommodate the few magazines/couple of books.

For this initiative, plan to set aside roughly 2–3 hours from start to finish.

Macramé Materials Needed

- 12" Wooden Dowel/Rod
- 3mm Single Strand Cotton Cord

Length of Cords

- 24 x 300cm strands of cord

Macramé Garland

You will begin to note that some large macramé components get more complicated and complex to create as we proceed through macramé project ideas. You would need to configure a spacious and wide room to either allow you to stretch out or work on the piece or provide a rack that is large enough to carry the piece to work.

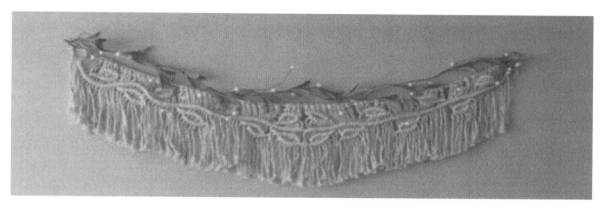

Fig: Macramé garland

If you live in a small living space, creating sufficient space can become tricky for us. On a wide dining room table beside a basket of our cords and supplies, we find that it is best to work in an open space. We also wish to work next to a window to get the sun's natural light and the sun's warmth shining on us. That makes for a workspace that is relaxing and pleasant.

That is the fairly long piece hanging above our fireplace right now. We used one knot for this project to form a bunch of leaf-shaped patterns throughout our project. The project took two hours or so from start to end.

Macramé Materials Needed

- 4mm Cotton Cord's spool

Length of Cords

- 60 x 80cm
- 4 x 60cm
- 2 x 120cm
- 10 x 100cm
- 1 x 155cm

Macramé Tote Bag

If you're looking for a pragmatic and sustainable project, the macramé net bag may be the perfect project for you.

Fig: Modern-day macramé-net tote bag

We made a macramé net bag ourselves at the start of this year. We are seeking to be more ecologically mindful of what we consume and what we use. We have tried to do our bit in the world to eliminate the use of plastic as soon as possible, and what better way than shopping bags for me to start.

This was a project where we, coupled with our passion for macramé, used some creativity and built something that would have an environmental impact. If you just want to reduce plastic bags and lean towards recycled bags, this is a wonderful idea that you can do. You will find that the spacing between the knots may be a little wide on this specific project, and it will fall out when putting any objects within. You should put a cloth bag alongside it to mitigate this so that the products do not spill out.

Creating handles and adding them to the bag is another area of difficulty that certain individuals frequently encounter.

Give this project a shot if you like the concept of combining art with a notable cause. The resources that you will need to help lead you are below.

Macramé Needed Materials

Small Size – 22cm wide & 44cm length (including handle)

- 4mm Single Strand Cotton Cord

Length of Cords

- 2 x 300cm
- 20 x 250cm
- 4 x 40cm

Medium Size – 30cm wide and 50cm length

- A spool of 4mm Single Strand Cotton Cord

Length of Cords

- 2 x 350cm
- 32 x 300cm
- 4 x 50cm

Macramé Bedroom Wall Hanging

It is where we get the most fun when making macramé to make larger designs that use several knots and be able to come with your special pattern. When you come up with the ideas and pursue them all the way, there is a very satisfying feeling you get. A deep feeling of pleasure and happiness remains.

Fig: Macramé wall hanging

For this macramé project, we decided to take a piece of antique macramé and convert it into modern home decor to hang over our headboard in our bedroom. We opted for a neutral beige cotton cord instead of using old, outdated colored thread. By using 6 knots- the Lark's Head knot, Clove Hitch knot, Berry knot, Josephine knot, Gathering knot, and Square knot, shaped the pattern to create this bedroom wall hanger (we find that the neutral beige cord suits our style).

You need the following items to start this project:

Macramé Materials Needed

- Wooden Dowel 36" inch length
- 4mm Single Strand Cotton Cord

Length of Cords

- 12 x 250cm
- 14 x 280cm
- 15 x 300cm

Macramé Lantern / Chandelier

We have now been reached our final project, i.e., a macramé lantern. We would strongly urge you to handle projects that will force you to come out of your comfort zone and try something new in macramé skill and take it to the next level.

To get better, learning and consistently creating is the best way.

Fig: Macramé chandelier

When we challenged ourselves to design and make a macramé lantern that was completely original and distinct from any other project that we had previously created, that is what we did.

This is an advanced project which took me a couple of hours to finish. Well, over 4 hours, so who keeps track.

Working with knots across the ring and making a 3-dimensional pattern is the challenging part of this project. All the macramé designs we shared above are 2-dimensional, all of which can be achieved for the flat laying project. You will continuously shift the project around, swap positions, and twist and transform as you create the pattern while working on the 3-dimensional

114

project. It is best to hang the workpiece on a revolving double-ended swivel ring hook for these kinds of tasks. This will make your life a lot simpler.

If you intend to build this or something similar, understanding what segment you are creating and not messing up the knot count while forming patterns is another place you should be careful. When planning to do this project, we made a few mistakes by not remembering the count of the knots for the pattern we were trying to make. We were compelled to go back a couple of steps to unravel and re-tie our knots.

You will deal with 5 knots for this project: the Gathering knot, Clove Hitch knot, Lark's Head knot, Berry knot, and Square knot. The project is very lengthy and with some difficulty, we suggest going slow and ensuring that any knot you make is aligned and right when moving along each part. Although this is an advanced project, don't be discouraged by how complicated it might look.

The second component of this project is that you can add to this macramé lantern on a larger bottom piece.

For this macramé lantern project, you'll need the following items and supplies.

Macramé Supplies Needed

- 16cm ring (wood or metal)
- 4mm Single Strand Cotton Cord

Length of Cords

- 8 x 100cm
- 40 x 200cm
- 1 x 60cm

Conclusion

You've worked hard to put together your first macramé project. You may be wondering what you can do with your skillset now that you've mastered the art of macramé. We're here to help, and before we go any further, keep in mind that while mastery of a craft doesn't equal financial freedom for those who practice it, it does give you enormous creative potential!

Our mission begins with a search for peace of mind, and we want to empower you to do what you love. It's these goals that drive us to share our experience and knowledge with others. Our strong passion for macramé shines through in every project we do and through our online resources, we hope to inspire as many people as possible to create beautiful things with their hands.

Macramé is a type of knotting and weaving art in which string, yarn, twine, or thread is threaded through a series of interlaced loops to make a picture. In our catalog, we provide a variety of macramé projects that are perfect for beginners. You can create simple decorative items or more complex items such as hanging decorations or jewelry pendants.

When you want something unique for your home, shop, or office, browse our macramé items and start creating your masterpiece today!

Macramé is one of several methods used to tie knots for decorative purposes. It originated in ancient Egypt and can be traced as far back as 3000 BC. The simplest form resembles an oversized knot tied in half-hitches, but macramé can be much more complicated. The word "macramé" is derived from the French word "machap" which translates roughly to "knot." Macramé has dozens of different techniques and uses depending on the kinds of materials used. The most popular forms are:

Classic Macramé – This is the kind of macramé that your granny taught you when she first stitched your initials into her apron. Classic Macramé tends to be quite heavy and bulky. It is known for its bright colors and beauty. However, it could use some modernizing if it's done this century!

Artistic Macramé – This involves macramé patterns that look like art, not necessarily decorations. Artistic Macramé can also be done without using knots, making it easier to learn than Classic Macramé. This kind of macramé allows the artist a lot more freedom so that they can really express their creativity and imagination through their work.

Macramé is a form of knot tying that originated in the Middle Ages, and it was used to create decorative items for special occasions. A macramé artist uses a variety of decorative thread and cords to create intricate ornaments, and it's a great way to add a bit of whimsy to your home decorations.

The first time you tie a macramé knot, it may seem like an impossible task. However, once you master the proper techniques, you'll be able to tie beautiful knots in no time!

A little macramé can go a long way when you want to create a beautiful piece of art. If you want to learn how, start with this practical guide! Once you've mastered the basics, you'll be well on your way to making timeless accessories that will last for generations to come.

We all know that macramé is so much more than just a simple knot. It is the perfect way of showing your love for the arts in a simple and easy-to-create way. A good macramé is the same way—it's as simple as the materials used with a little practice. With this guide, learning how to make macramé will become easier!

Printed in Great Britain
by Amazon